PLAY WITH FIRE
AND OTHER STORIES

based on the television series created by
JOSS WHEDON

by CHRISTOPHER GOLDEN

with Me, Play with Fire, and Stinger
CTOR GOMEZ & SANDU FLOREA

The Latest Craze
written by TOM SNIEGOSKI
IFF RICHARDS & JOE PIMENTEL

Letters by CLEM ROBINS & KEN BRUZENAK

Colors by GUY MAJOR

Cover photo by KEITH WOOD

These stories take place during Buffy the Vampire Slayer's third season.

DARK HORSE COMICS®

Dance with Me

PLAY WITH FIRE

THERE HAS BEEN A GREAT DEAL OF VAMPIRE ACTIVITY HERE, OF LATE. BUFFY SUMMERS, THE CHOSEN ONE, HAS COME TO INVESTIGATE.

I WONDER IF YOU AREN'T RUSHING THINGS A BIT.

NO RUSHING. HONEST. I'M BEING REALLY CAREFUL.

I SHOULD HOPE SO, WILLOW. MAGIC IS NOT A FORCE TO BE TAKEN LIGHTLY.

I DON'T, GILES, I TAKE IT... HEAVILY. OR NOT LIGHTLY. I HAVE MY SERIOUS FACE ON WHEN THE WITCHIN' HOUR COMES. REALLY.

INDEED. YET I DON'T THINK I NEED TO REMIND YOU THAT YOUR SPELLS HAVE NOT ALWAYS GONE AS PLANNED. IN SPELL-CASTING, THE TINIEST MISTAKE COULD LEAD TO --

DISASTER. RIGHT. I KNOW. BUT I'M GOOD AT THIS, GILES. AND THE ONLY WAY I CAN LEARN IS BY DOING.

I'M MERELY OBSERVING THAT PERHAPS IT'S TIME FOR ME TO DO A BIT OF AN AUDIT, SIT IN ON A FEW SPELLS, PERHAPS OFFER SUGGESTIONS.

I DON'T THINK I -- WHAT? YOU WOULD? WANT TO, I MEAN? I WOULD HAVE ASKED, BUT YOU'RE ALWAYS SO BUSY, WHAT WITH BEING THE WATCHER AND --

THE WATCHER. RIGHT. SO HOW 'BOUT MORE WATCHING AND LESS CHITTY-CHATTING? IT'S LIKE HUNTING VAMPIRES WITH REGIS AND KATHIE LEE.

NOW LOOK AROUND. WITH ALL THE ATTACKS LATELY, THIS PLACE SHOULD BE VAMP CENTRAL.

TRY LOOKING BEHIND YOU!

BUFFY!

THE WEATHERMAN DIDN'T SAY ANYTHING ABOUT IT RAINING VAMPIRES TODAY, DID HE?

GET OFF HER, YOU...YOU... BLOODSUCKING FREAKS!

UGH, WILL. I HATED THAT MOVIE. BUT, OKAY, ACCURATE.

NOW LISTEN, BOYS, THIS ISN'T A WAY TO GET A DATE. YOU'VE REALLY GOTTA LEARN TO GIVE A GIRL A LITTLE...

SPACE!

GOOD ONE, GILES.

HMM...WHAT? OH, INDEED. WELL THEN...

DON'T GET TOO WILD WITH ENTHUSIASM, GILES. THERE ARE STILL...UHNFF... STILL TWO OF THEM GETTING AWAY.

THEY'RE HEADING FOR THAT OLD HOUSE.

WE MUSTN'T LET THEM ESCAPE.

DON'T WORRY, THEY'RE NOT GETTING OUT OF HERE.

COULD I JUST NOTE THAT THIS PLACE SEEMS ABANDONED AND, OKAY, APPROPRIATELY SPOOKY?

RELAX, WILL. THOSE VAMPS ARE ABOUT TO FIND OUT THAT THE MOST DANGER-OUS THING IN THIS PLACE IS ME.

OH, COME ON! VAMPIRES AREN'T SUPPOSED TO HIDE, THEY'RE SUPPOSED TO ATTACK.

I HAVE A TRIG TEST IN THE MORNING, GUYS, HELP ME OUT HERE.

QUICKLY, TO THE ATTIC.

BUMMP!

C'MON. I HEARD SOMETHING UPSTAIRS.

DO BE CAREFUL, BUFFY. I FIND IT DIFFICULT TO BELIEVE THAT EVEN THE STUPIDEST VAMPIRE WOULD RETREAT TO SOME-WHERE FROM WHICH THEY COULD NOT ESCAPE.

SAY, ARE WE SURE THIS PLACE IS ABANDONED? I HAVE THAT WEIRD, CREEPY, SOMEBODY'S-WATCHING-ME FEELING.

I THINK I HEARD SOMETHING ABOVE US. THERE MUST BE ANOTHER SET OF STAIRS.

SEE, GILES, YOU GIVE THE BLOODSUCKERS TOO MUCH CREDIT. ONLY A MORON WOULD HIDE IN THE ATTIC. IT'S THE ULTIMATE NO-RETREAT RETREAT.

OKAY! HOW WAS I SUPPOSED TO KNOW THEY HAD A WHOLE NEST GOING ON UP THERE?

WILLOW, FOR GOD'S SAKE, GET BACK! WE'VE GOT TO HAVE ROOM TO DEFEND OURSELVES.

UM, GUYS...

OH, BOY.

HI, MY NAME'S BRYAN. WHAT'S YOURS?

OH, I'M, UM, WILLOW. AND GILES. I MEAN, THIS IS GILES.

HEY, WILL! COULD WE FLIRT WITH THE GHOST-BOY WHEN WE'RE DONE FIGHTING FOR OUR LIVES, PLEASE? I COULD USE A LITTLE--HEY!

IT'S SO NICE TO HAVE SOME HUMAN COMPANY. IT'S BEEN QUITE SOME TIME SINCE--

OH, EXCUSE ME.

IT ISN'T THAT I'M AGAINST SOCIALIZING, SEE...

I WASN'T FLIRTING.

OH, WOW, I'M SORRY. I'M PROBABLY BEING A DISTRACTION. IT'S JUST BEEN SO LONG...

I'M BEING RUDE, AREN'T I? YOU GUYS WOULD PROBABLY LIKE SOME HELP.

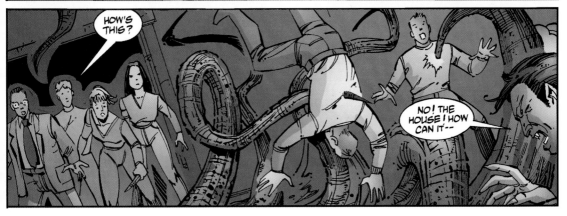

HOW'S THIS?

NO! THE HOUSE! HOW CAN IT--

THAT WAS NOT BAD, ACTUALLY. ≷COUGH COUGH≷ THANKS FOR THE HELP. MAYBE I CAN ACTUALLY GET HOME IN TIME TO STUDY FOR THAT TRIG TEST NOW.

I'M SORRY, BUT I DON'T THINK I CAN LET YOU LEAVE.

"IT WAS THE SPRING OF '88. I WAS SIXTEEN. A BUNCH OF US HAD STARTED TO DABBLE IN MAGIC AND STUFF. I THOUGHT IT WOULD BE COOL IF WE TRIED TO RAISE A DEMON.

"I DON'T THINK WE RAISED ANYTHING, BUT WE DID SOMETHING TO THE HOUSE, BROUGHT IT TO LIFE SOMEHOW.

"THE OTHERS ALL GOT AWAY. THEY DIDN'T EVEN LOOK BACK. THE HOUSE HAD ME--TOOK ME AND MADE ME A PART OF IT."

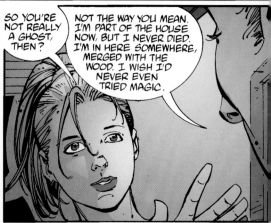

SO YOU'RE NOT REALLY A GHOST, THEN?

NOT THE WAY YOU MEAN. I'M PART OF THE HOUSE NOW, BUT I NEVER DIED. I'M IN HERE SOMEWHERE, MERGED WITH THE WOOD. I WISH I'D NEVER EVEN TRIED MAGIC.

THAT SOUNDS A LOT LIKE YOUR CUE, WILLOW. THINK YOU CAN GET HIM OUT?

WELL, SINCE YOU ASKED--

NO.

WE CAN'T BE CERTAIN HE'S TELLING THE TRUTH ABOUT ANY OF THIS.

BUT...WHAT IF HE IS, AND WE JUST LEAVE HIM HERE? I'D NEVER BE ABLE TO SLEEP AGAIN, GILES.

COME ON, GILES, YOU'RE HERE TO SUPERVISE. AND IF YOU'RE RIGHT AND HE'S EVIL, I'M HERE TO KICK HIS LYING BUTT.

...ALL RIGHT, BUT WE MUST BE VERY CAREFUL.

A STANDARD EXORCISM SHOULD BE ABLE TO DRIVE THE ENTITY OUT OF THE HOUSE, AND BRYAN SHOULD BE FREE.

SHOULD?

"BE THOU DEMON, FIEND, OR SORCERER, THOU HAST INVADED THIS HOUSE. LET THY EVIL RECEDE FROM THIS HOUSE INTO THY MARROW AND INTO THY BONE. LET IT BE NOW WITHDRAWN."

DO YOU THINK IT'S GOING TO WORK?

WELL, IT CERTAINLY SEEMS TO BE DOING SOMETHING.

um, WILLOW? MAYBE YOU SHOULD HURRY.

WILLOW, SPEED IT UP, PLEASE!

NO! NOOO!

"LET THY EVIL RECEDE FROM THIS HOUSE INTO THY MARROW AND INTO THY BONE. LET IT BE NOW WITHDRAWN."

HELP MEEEE!

DAMN, IT ISN'T WORKING, BUFFY, WE'VE GOT TO TRY SOMETHING ELSE.

GIVE HER A CHANCE, GILES.

"I EXORCISE THEE FOR THE SAKE OF THIS HOUSE."

WILLOW!

"I COMMAND THEE TO DEPART!"

IT WORKED. YAY, ME. NOT THAT I'M, Y'KNOW, BRAGGING OR ANYTHING.

UHNFF!

YOU HAVE EVERY RIGHT TO BRAG, WILLOW. YOU'VE GIVEN ME MY LIFE BACK.

IT FEELS WEIRD, BEING OLD. I MEAN, OLDER, Y'KNOW. BUT THAT'S NOTHING COMPARED TO BEING ALIVE AGAIN, ABLE TO BREATHE AND WALK. THANK YOU ALL SO MUCH.

ESPECIALLY YOU, WILLOW. GOODBYE.

SO, DO YOU THINK HIS FAMILY WILL BUY THAT WHOLE ABDUCTED-BY-ALIENS THING?

I SUSPECT THEY'LL BE PLEASED SIMPLY TO TO HAVE HIM BACK.

YEAH, PLUS, Y'KNOW, SUNNYDALE.

YOU'VE GOTTA ADMIT, GILES, WILLOW'S "DABBLING" CAME IN PRETTY HANDY.

INDEED. HOWEVER, WE CAN'T FORGET--

DON'T WORRY. I'M SURE SHE'D BE THRILLED TO GET SOME POINTERS FROM YOU. AND WHILE YOU'RE HELPING HER, MAYBE I CAN GO OUT ON A DATE ONCE IN A WHILE.

LET'S NOT GET CARRIED AWAY.

THE END

THEY SAY WAR IS HELL. SO IS HIGH SCHOOL. AND IN THE CASE OF SUNNYDALE HIGH, WELL, THE SCHOOL IS BUILT RIGHT ON TOP OF THE "BOCA DEL INFIERNO."

THE HELLMOUTH.

SO, XANDER, ARE YOU GOING TO THE GAME TONIGHT, OR JUST MEETING CORDELIA AFTER?

BUT, Y'KNOW, ASIDE FROM THAT? IT'S PRETTY MUCH LIKE EVERY OTHER SCHOOL.

ACTUALLY, I WAS KIND OF THINKING--

ABOUT GOING TO THE [LIB]RARY. NOW. 'CUZ WE [L]OVE IT THERE SO VERY MUCH.

HEY, ROSENBERG, WAIT UP!

OH, HEY, JOE! LOOK, XANDER, IT'S JOE.

I'VE CALLED YOU LIKE THREE TIMES, WILLOW, AND YOU'RE MAJORLY BLOWING ME OFF. I NEED MATH HELP, OR I'M GONNA FAIL. I FAIL, I CAN'T PLAY FOOT-BALL. I DON'T PLAY, WE LOSE!

BACK OFF, BURGESS! MAN, NOT TOO FULL OF YOUR-SELF, ARE YOU?

HAS IT OCCURRED TO YOUR NEANDERTHAL BRAIN THAT WILLOW'S TRYING TO GET OUT OF TUTORING BECAUSE YOU'RE, OH, I DON'T KNOW, A JERK? NOT TO MENTION RATHER LARGE AND SCARY?

THAT'S IT, HARRIS! I'VE AVOIDED KICKING YOUR BUTT FOR YEARS, MAINLY BECAUSE EVERYONE ELSE HAD BEEN THERE FIRST. BUT NOW YOU'VE STEPPED IN IT, LOSER.

TONIGHT. AFTER THE GAME. UNDER THE AWAY TEAM BLEACHERS.

I'LL BE THERE, NUMB-SKULL!

STINGER

CRUEL. DELISSSHULISS.

IT HATES THE SUN. MUCH NICER IN THE COOL, DARK PLACE WHERE IT SLEPT. BUT WHEN IT GOT THE SCENT... THE CRUEL SCENT... IT HAD TO COME UP AND SEE. THERE WILL BE A HUNT COME NIGHTFALL. WHEN THE SHADOWS WILL HIDE IT.

OH GOD, OH GOD...YOU'LL COME TO MY FUNERAL, RIGHT WILL?

OF COURSE I WILL, XANDER... WELL, NO. I MEAN, I WOULD IF YOU WERE GOING TO HAVE A FUNERAL. WHICH YOU'RE NOT.

'CAUSE YOU CAN'T FIGHT HIM... YOU DO KNOW THAT, RIGHT?

OH, SURE, YOU SAY THAT NOW. BUT NO, ACTUALLY, YOU'RE WRONG, SEE. I CAN FIGHT HIM. I JUST CAN'T BEAT HIM.

HEY! GOOD NEWS, BOYS AND GIRLS! NO SLAYING TONIGHT. I'M GOING TO PRETEND TO BE A REAL HIGH SCHOOL KID, WHO'S GOING TO THE GAME?

...MAYBE IF I GO TO MEXICO FOR A FEW YEARS, HE'LL FORGET ABOUT IT...HE ISN'T ALL THAT BRIGHT...

WELL, I WAS GOING TO GO WATCH THE DINGOES PLAY AT THE BRONZE, BUT...OKAY. XANDER'S GOING TO FIGHT JOE BURGESS AFTER THE GAME TONIGHT.

WHAT?

XANDER, ARE YOU OUT OF YOUR MIND?

WOW. IF ROCKY HAD YOU IN HIS CORNER, THEY'D STILL BE MAKING SEQUELS.

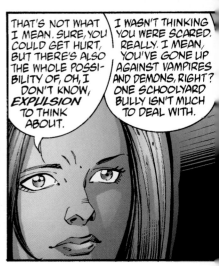

THAT'S NOT WHAT I MEAN. SURE, YOU COULD GET HURT, BUT THERE'S ALSO THE WHOLE POSSI- BILITY OF, OH, I DON'T KNOW, EXPULSION TO THINK ABOUT.

I WASN'T THINKING YOU WERE SCARED, REALLY. I MEAN, YOU'VE GONE UP AGAINST VAMPIRES AND DEMONS, RIGHT? ONE SCHOOLYARD BULLY ISN'T MUCH TO DEAL WITH.

BURGESS IS BIG AND UGLY, BUFFY, BUT IN CASE YOU MISSED IT, HE'S HUMAN. MUCH AS I'D LIKE TO, I CAN'T PUT A STAKE THROUGH HIM, Y'KNOW. THIS IS THE REAL WORLD.

SEE YA LATER, GUYS. GOTTA WORK ON MY WILL. JUST SO YOU KNOW, I'D LIKE MY ASHES SCATTERED AT SEA.

HE'S AFRAID.

VERY. HE'D BE STUPID NOT TO BE. JOE'S GOING TO KILL HIM.

LATER, AFTER THE GAME...

Y'KNOW, JOE, WE COULD AVOID UNPLEASANTRY AND BLOODSHED AND SETTLE THIS IN A MORE MANLY TRADITION...WITH AN OLD-FASHIONED CHUTES AND LADDERS TOUR-NAMENT! ...NAH, HE'LL NEVER GO FOR THAT... MAYBE PICTIONARY...NO SPELLING REQUIRED THERE...

OKAY, JOE, I'M HERE AND YOU AREN'T...YOU FOR-FEIT, RIGHT? I'M LEAVING NOW...

YOU HARRIS?

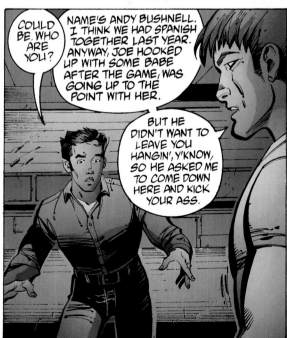

COULD BE. WHO ARE YOU?

NAME'S ANDY BUSHNELL. I THINK WE HAD SPANISH TOGETHER LAST YEAR. ANYWAY, JOE HOOKED UP WITH SOME BABE AFTER THE GAME, WAS GOING UP TO THE POINT WITH HER.

BUT HE DIDN'T WANT TO LEAVE YOU HANGIN', Y'KNOW, SO HE ASKED ME TO COME DOWN HERE AND KICK YOUR ASS.

YOU GUYS GET TO GILES, TELL HIM WHAT'S GOING ON, THEN MEET ME AT THE POINT.

THOUGHT YOU'D NEVER ASK.

HMM. RATHER LOW ON CROSSBOW BOLTS. PERHAPS I OUGHT TO SPRING FOR A GROSS THIS TIME, TO SAVE ON SHIPPING IN THE--

GILES!

WE'VE GOT A MONSTER OR DEMON ON THE PROWL. BUFFY THINKS IT'S HUNTING JOE BURGESS, AND SHE'S GONE UP TO THE POINT TO TRY TO KILL THE THING!

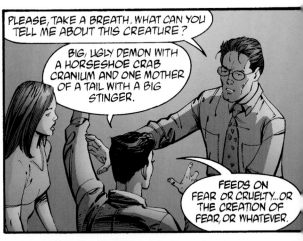

PLEASE, TAKE A BREATH. WHAT CAN YOU TELL ME ABOUT THIS CREATURE?

BIG, UGLY DEMON WITH A HORSESHOE CRAB CRANIUM AND ONE MOTHER OF A TAIL WITH A BIG STINGER.

FEEDS ON FEAR OR CRUELTY...OR THE CREATION OF FEAR, OR WHATEVER.

FEEDS ON...WELL, I'LL BE. I NEVER THOUGHT THE DAY WOULD COME.

WOW, GILES. PREPARED BOY. BRINGS NEW MEANING TO THE OLD SAYING, "IF I KNEW YOU WERE COMING, I'D HAVE BAKED A CAKE."

JUST DOING INVENTORY, ACTUALLY. AS TO THIS MONSTER, HOWEVER, WHEN MY GRANDMOTHER WAS A WATCHER, SHE AND HER SLAYER FACED A CREATURE SIMILAR TO WHAT YOU DESCRIBE.

THEY BARELY ESCAPED WITH THEIR LIVES.

THANKS FOR THE PEP TALK, GILES. CAN WE GO BACK BUFFY UP, NOW?

DID IT LOOK SOMETHING LIKE THIS?

IT LOOKED EXACTLY LIKE THAT.

SO CAN WE KILL IT NOW, OR WHAT?

THEY USED TO CALL IT "MAKEOUT POINT," BUT NOBODY CAN SAY THAT NAME WITH A STRAIGHT FACE ANYMORE. NOW IT'S JUST "THE POINT."

OH, JOE, I COULDN'T BELIEVE YOU RAN THAT TOUCHDOWN IN. YOU MUST HAVE SO MANY BRUISES.

I CAN TAKE IT, BABE. IT AIN'T ANY FUN IF YOU DON'T GET A LITTLE BIT BLACK AND BLUE.

NOK NOK

WHO THE...?

HUH? WHAT THE HELL DO YOU WANT?

OUT OF THE CAR, BURGESS. WE NEED TO TALK.

I'M GOING TO FIND A NICE SPOT TO RETCH. HER? I DON'T MIND BEING THE OTHER WOMAN, JOE, BUT *NOT* TO *BUFFY SUMMERS.* I THINK I NEED TO LOOFAH WITH BRILLO.

NO, HEY, HARMONY! HOLD UP! I WOULDN'T GO NEAR THIS PSYCHO FOR AN *NFL* CONTRACT.

THANKS A LOT, YOU CRAZY DITZ. WHAT'D I EVER DO TO YOU?

WELL, NOT THAT YOUR STEROIDS DESERVE SAVING, BUT...I'D RUN IF I WERE YOU.

HUNGREEEE!

GET OUT OF THE CAR, PINHEAD!

HUNGREEEE!

FFEARRR.

HEY, HANDSOME, WHERE YA GOING? WOW, I DON'T KNOW WHETHER TO BE RELIEVED OR INSULTED.

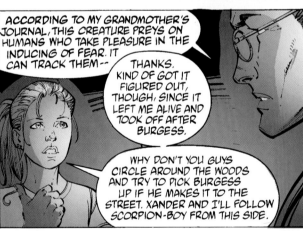

BUFFY, ARE YOU ALL RIGHT?

I'LL BE DUCKY. GIVE ME A MINUTE TO CATCH MY BREATH. AND STOP BLEEDING.

OH, NO... IT STUNG YOU?

I MUST SAY, I'M ASTONISHED THAT EVEN A SLAYER COULD SURVIVE THAT DEMON'S ATTACK.

THANKS, I GUESS.

ACCORDING TO MY GRANDMOTHER'S JOURNAL, THIS CREATURE PREYS ON HUMANS WHO TAKE PLEASURE IN THE INDUCING OF FEAR. IT CAN TRACK THEM--

THANKS. KIND OF GOT IT FIGURED OUT, THOUGH, SINCE IT LEFT ME ALIVE AND TOOK OFF AFTER BURGESS.

WHY DON'T YOU GUYS CIRCLE AROUND THE WOODS AND TRY TO PICK BURGESS UP IF HE MAKES IT TO THE STREET. XANDER AND I'LL FOLLOW SCORPION-BOY FROM THIS SIDE.

I'M NOT SURE I FEEL LIKE SAVING JOE BURGESS'S LIFE, BUFFY.

I'M SURE YOU DON'T. BUT THAT'S THE POINT, RIGHT? THAT'S WHAT SEPARATES US FROM THE DEMONS. FROM PEOPLE LIKE BURGESS, TOO.

KARAK

Uh-uh. THAT WORKED ONCE. DO I LOOK STUPID TO YOU?

SHUNNK!

YOU LOOK LIKE DESSERT TO HIM.

WHAT DOES IT TAKE TO STOP YOU, DEMON?

SNAPP!

SSSSSS

OKAY, MORE THAN THAT, APPARENTLY.

WHAT ABOUT...

CHUK

WOW, G-MAN. YOU'RE PRETTY GOOD WITH THAT THING. EVER DO ANY BEHEADING IN YOUR WILD YOUTH?

I SUPPOSE I'LL TAKE THAT AS A "THANK YOU." AND I'VE TOLD YOU NEVER TO CALL ME THAT.

THANKS, XANDER. THAT WAS A NASTY LITTLE DEMON. IT AMAZES ME THAT YOU CAN FIGHT SOMETHING LIKE THAT, AND STILL BE AFRAID OF A GUY LIKE JOE BURGESS.

I KNOW. KIND OF A WIMP, HUH?

XANDER, REALLY. THERE'S NO SHAME IN BEING AFRAID OF PAIN AND HUMILIATION.

WHAT TAKES REAL COURAGE IS KNOWING WHEN TO FIGHT AND WHEN TO WALK AWAY...HEY, WILLOW, WHERE'S JOE?

I ASKED HIM IF HE STILL WANTED TO FIGHT XANDER. Y'KNOW, AFTER YOU GUYS WERE DONE KILLING THE MONSTER HE WAS RUNNING AWAY FROM? HE KIND OF TOOK OFF AFTER THAT.

YOU'RE KIDDING? THAT MUSCLEBOUND, STEROID-HEAD IS AFRAID OF ME?

I'M TELLING YOU GUYS, THIS TOWN GETS WEIRDER EVERY DAY.

HEY!

THE END

SLAYER!!!

WHERE IS SHE? I WILL SPARE THE LIFE OF THE FIRST TO SPEAK. TELL ME WHERE THE SLAYER HAS GONE.

SPIRITS OF THE STORM, PROTECT YOUR SUPPLICANTS! WE BOW BEFORE THEE, CRADLED IN THE SILENCE OF YOUR EYE!

THAT OUGHTTA DO IT.

YOU KNOW, YOU'RE KINDA CUTE WHEN YOU'RE SPELLCASTING.

HAVE YOU CHECKED THE CUSHIONS ON THE SOFA? I'M ALWAYS LOSING STUFF DOWN THERE.

XANDER, NOW'S NOT THE TIME. AND HE DOES HAVE A POINT. IT WOULD BE HELPFUL TO KNOW JUST WHERE BUFFY HAS GOTTEN OFF TO.

BUFFY SUMMERS KIND OF LIKES THE RAIN. WHEN YOU LIVE IN SOUTHERN CALIFORNIA, IT'S SORT OF A NOVELTY. STORY OF HER LIFE...

SNAP

ANYTHING SHE LIKES, EVEN THE SMALLEST THING, EVENTUALLY SOME DEMON HAS TO COME ALONG AND SCREW IT UP.

WHERE IS THE SLAYER?!

OKAY, THE TOY WAS *NOT* LOOKING AT ME.

HE WAS KIND OF CUTE, THOUGH.

"THIS ISN'T LIKE YOU, WILLOW. YOU'RE A BRIGHT GIRL. WHY WOULD YOU SPEND ALL THAT MONEY ON SOMETHING SO RIDICULOUSLY IMPRACTICAL?"

OH, SO I'M RIDICULOUS NOW? THANKS SO MUCH. WELL YOU KNOW WHAT? IT'S MY MONEY, MOM, AND I'LL SPEND IT IF I WANT TO!

FINE. BUT YOU'RE GOING TO FEEL AWFULLY SILLY WHEN THIS LITTLE FAD IS OVER.

IT'S *NOT* A FAD!

SLAM

WOW. OKAY, TEENAGE DAUGHTER EQUALS REBELLION, BUT...

WOW. WHERE DID THAT COME FROM?

YOU'RE THE ONLY ONE WHO UNDERSTANDS ME, ALEISTER.

THOUGH SHE HAS ACCEPTED HER ROLE AS THE CHOSEN ONE, NOT A DAY GOES BY THAT BUFFY DOESN'T FEEL SOME REGRET ABOUT THE PIECES OF NORMAL TEENAGE LIFE THAT SHE'S MISSED.

THE DARKNESS SHE FACES EACH DAY NEVER FAILS TO INTRUDE ON A DATE OR A DANCE OR A FOOTBALL GAME. ON THE OTHER HAND, THERE ARE SOME THINGS SHE'S GLAD TO MISS.

BUFFY SUMMERS DOESN'T HAVE TIME TO WORRY ABOUT THE LATEST CRAZE.

SO WHAT YOU'RE SAYING IS YOU ACTUALLY HIT THE SACK BEFORE LETTERMAN?

THREE NIGHTS IN A ROW. I HAVEN'T SEEN HIDE NOR HAIR OF ANYTHING THAT WOULD EVEN BE TEMPTED TO GO BUMP IN THE NIGHT. MAYBE THERE'S A CONVENTION OUT OF TOWN?

OR SOMEBODY PAINTED "HOME OF THE SLAYER" ON THE WELCOME TO SUNNYDALE SIGN.

YOU'RE GIVING THEM TOO MUCH CREDIT. THE FORCES OF DARKNESS ARE NOT KNOWN FOR THEIR SMARTS.

I GUESS I'M JUST STARTING TO GET ANTSY. WHAT GOOD'S A SLAYER WITHOUT SOMETHING TO SLAY?

OH, I'D SAY THERE ARE LOADS OF THINGS WE CAN FIND FOR SOMEONE OF YOUR SPECIAL TALENTS TO DO.

HEY GUYS. EVERYONE READY FOR THE HISTORY TEST? I'M KINDA STOKED.

I DON'T THINK I'D EVER USE "STOKED" AND "TEST" IN THE SAME SENTENCE, BUT I THINK I'M SET. WHO'S YOUR LITTLE FRIEND?

THIS IS ALEISTER! HE'S MY--

--HOOLIGAN. OH, PLEASE, WILLOW, COME ON. BETTER TO BE HOOLIGAN-LESS THAN TO BUY THE BOTTOM OF THE LINE.

WHAT'S THE MATTER, CORDY? GETTING ALL I'LL-GET-YOU-MY-PRETTY JUST 'CAUSE YOU WERE SNOOZIN' WHEN THE FAD TRAIN PULLED INTO TOWN?

HE'S CUTE, IN AN UGLY KIND OF WAY. I HOPE THAT'S NOT MY COMPETITION.

I'LL TELL YOU WHAT'S UGLY. ALL THE LITTLE ACCESSORIES THEY HAVE FOR THESE THINGS AT HOOLIGAN HOVEL, THEY'LL JUST MILK EVERY DOLLAR OUT OF IT UNTIL IT DIES.

AND ANYWAY, IT'S ONLY WORTH HAVING ONE IF YOU HAVE THE MOST EXPENSIVE ONE, A PLATINUM LIMITED EDITION. WHICH, OF COURSE, I HAVE ON ORDER AS WE SPEAK.

OF COURSE YOU--

YOU SNOOZE, YOU LOSE, MORON. THEY ONLY HAD ONE HOOLIGAN LIKE THIS, AND I WAS GONNA HAVE IT. IT WAS WORTH THE THREE HUNDRED DOLLARS JUST TO SEE HOW JEALOUS EVERYONE IS.

YOU DON'T GET IT! I WAS SAVING UP. THAT'S A PLATINUM LIMITED EDITION.

THREE HUNDRED DOLLARS? EVERYTHING I OWN DOESN'T ADD UP TO THREE HUNDRED DOLLARS.

AND YOU WERE GONNA SPEND THAT ON A DOLL?

NOT THAT THERE'S ANYTHING WRONG WITH THAT.

MAYBE THEY STILL HAVE ONE OF THE FOOTBALL HOOLIGANS, YEAH, THAT'D BE COOL.

PLATINUM, HUH? I HAVE ONE OF THE TITANIUM EDITIONS ON ORDER.

AM I THE ONLY ONE WHO THOUGHT THAT WAS A BIT STRANGE?

IF YOUR DEFINITION OF "A BIT STRANGE" INCLUDES HAVING EVERYTHING YOU THOUGHT YOU UNDERSTOOD THRASHED WITHIN AN INCH OF ITS LIFE ...THEN NO, YOU'RE NOT THE ONLY ONE.

I'M SORRY, GUYS... CRYING IS SO EMBARRASSING, AND MESSY. BUT MY GRANDMOTHER GAVE ME THAT BRACELET. IT'S THE ONLY THING I HAVE OF HERS, AND NOW IT'S JUST GONE...

YOU'LL FIND IT, ELISSA. AND, LOOK ON THE BRIGHT SIDE. AT LEAST YOU'VE STILL GOT JEREMY TO CHEER YOU UP.

YEAH. GUESS YOU'RE RIGHT. ;SNIFF; I DON'T KNOW WHAT I'D DO WITHOUT HIM. OKAY, CORDELIA'S NEW ONE MAY BE MORE EXPENSIVE -- THE WITCH -- BUT JEREMY JUST MAKES EVERYTHING OKAY.

HE'S THE ONLY ONE WHO UNDERSTANDS. IT'S LIKE MAGIC...

WHAT'S THE MATTER WITH YOU? I ASKED FOR A CHILI DOG. I DIDN'T ASK YOU TO SPLATTER CHILI ON THELONIUS! THE SCHOOL IS GOING TO PAY TO REPLACE HIM!

ALL I WANTED WAS A CHILI DOG...

SOMEONE WOKE UP CRANKY.

APPARENTLY, SOMEONE IS SUFFERING FROM CAFETERIA AMNESIA. ASKING FOR THIS STUFF IS A LITTLE LIKE ELECTIVE SURGERY.

HI, GUYS.

HEY, I'M WITNESSING SAD FACE. WHAT'S UP?

I ALMOST DON'T WANT TO TELL YOU, BUT... PEZ-WITCH IS GONE.

I'M SURE IT'LL TURN UP, WILL. SHE DIDN'T JUST UP AND FLY AWAY. NOT UNLESS SHE COMES WITH A PEZ BROOMSTICK.

IT'S OKAY.

I KNOW. OKAY, CANDY AND PLASTIC. BUT IT WAS THE FIRST THING YOU EVER GAVE ME AND, WELL, SENTIMENTAL VALUE AND ALL.

IF IT IS LOST, WE CAN ALWAYS GET YOU ANOTHER ONE.

OR, Y'KNOW, SOMETHING ELSE EQUALLY COOL. LIKE MAYBE A COMPLETE SET OF HOLOGRAPHIC, CHROME HOOLIGAN TRADING CARDS.

ALSO NICE. THEN AGAIN THERE'S THAT APPOINTMENT WITH THE PSYCHIATRIST YOU SO DESPERATELY NEED.

HOT PANTS.

THIS MUST BE THE PLACE.

HI! WELCOME TO HOOLIGAN HOVEL, THE AUTHORIZED CARRIER OF ALL THINGS HOOLIGAN. ARE YOU LOOKING FOR SOMETHING SPECIAL FOR YOUR LITTLE FRIEND?

UHH.... YEAH.

YOU'RE IN LUCK! WE JUST GOT A SHIPMENT OF NEW MERCHANDISE, INCLUDING HOOLIGAN BUBBLE BATH, THE HOOLIGAN DENTISTRY KIT--TO KEEP THOSE CHOPPERS SHINY, AND THE HOOLIGAN BEACH HOVEL WITH REAL WORKING JACUZZI. IT'S AWESOME.

EVERYBODY WHO'S ANYONE IS BUYING IT. AND IF YOU'RE LOOKING FOR THE LATEST IN HOOLIGAN FASHIONS--

I'D HAVE TO BE RICH. DO PEOPLE REALLY PAY THESE PRICES FOR ALL THIS STUFF WITHOUT YOU HOLDING A GUN TO THEIR HEADS?

OH, YOU'D BE SURPRISED. HOOLIGANS JUST MAKE PEOPLE HAPPY. AND MOST OF THESE ITEMS ARE LIMITED EDITION COLLECTIBLES, NOT AVAILABLE AT ANY OTHER STORE. IT'S AWESOME.

YEAH. AWESOME.

APPARENTLY, I'M THE ONLY ONE IN TOWN WHO THINKS YOU'RE AN UGLY, CREEPY LITTLE THING.

OKAY, HAVE AN AWESOME DAY! THANKS FOR STOPPING BY HOOLIGAN HOVEL, THE AUTHORIZED CARRIER OF ALL THINGS HOOLIGAN!

YOU CAN COME OUT NOW, BOSS. SHE'S GONE. I DIDN'T THINK SHE WAS MEAN, THOUGH. I THOUGHT SHE WAS KIND OF NICE. SHE HAD A CUTE HOOLIGAN...

WOULD YOU CEASE YOUR INANE PRATTLING, AND GET BACK TO STOCKING THE SHELVES?!

SURE THING, MR. RAYNE, RIGHT AWAY.

DON'T TOUCH MY HOOLIGAN, YOU FREAK! YOU WANT ONE, BUY ONE!

HOOLIGAN NIGHT
BRING YOUR HOOLIGAN DRINKS 1/2 PRICE

WOULD YOU BELIEVE AURA DOESN'T EVEN HAVE A HOOLIGAN?

SHE'S A CULTURAL CRIPPLE. SHE'S STILL TRYING TO KEEP THAT KEYCHAIN THING ALIVE.

DOES ANYONE ELSE FEEL LIKE WE'RE AT ZOMBIE FAIR '99? I DON'T KNOW, MAYBE I'M HALLUCINATING, BUT EVERYONE'S ACTING KINDA FUNKY.

YEAH, LAST I CHECKED, BRINGING YOUR TOYS TO THE LOCAL HOT SPOT WASN'T PART OF THE REPERTOIRE OF COOL.

SEE, NOW YOU'RE SCARING ME, 'CAUSE THAT'S JUST WHAT I WAS THINKING. COLOR ME CRAZY, BUT SEEMS TO ME ONLY THE POPULAR KIDS ARE ACTING WEIRD. POPULAR MEANING RICH.

RICH MEANING, "NOW OWNS A HOOLIGAN." I'M WILLING TO BET ALL THE WACKINESS HAS SOMETHING TO DO WITH THE UGLY LITTLE THINGS.

HOW CAN YOU EVEN SAY THAT? THAT'S SO... NOT NICE!

WILLOW'S NOT POPULAR OR RICH, SO THERE! YOU'RE JUST JEALOUS 'CAUSE YOU CAN'T AFFORD ONE.

YEAH, COR, THAT'S EXACTLY IT. ON THE NOSE. ACTUALLY, THOUGH, I DO HAVE ONE. DON'T KNOW WHERE I GOT IT, BUT--

SO YOU HAVE ONE, AND YOU'RE NOT ACTING AS PETTY AND COMPULSIVE AND... OKAY, I'LL SAY IT, OBSESSED... AS CERTAIN OTHER PEOPLE WE KNOW.

I MEAN, SOMEONE STEALS PEZ-WITCH AND CHROMIUM HOOLIGAN CARDS ARE A SUITABLE REPLACEMENT? WHAT'S UP WITH THAT?

WHAT, NOW YOU'RE JUDGING WHETHER OR NOT I GRIEVED ENOUGH FOR PEZ-WITCH? YOU THINK ALEISTER HAS SOME KIND OF MAGICAL HOLD ON ME OR SOMETHING?

PRETTY MUCH. YEP.

THAT'S RIDICULOUS! BUFFY HAS A HOOLIGAN, AND SHE'S BEEN WHINING ABOUT LOSING THAT CHEAP LITTLE RING ANGEL GAVE HER EVER SINCE WE GOT IN HERE.

I WAS GONNA SAY THAT.

TRUE, BUT BUFFY'S ALSO THE SLAYER. IF THESE THINGS ARE MAKING EVERYONE ACT FREAKY, MAYBE THEY CAN'T AFFECT HER.

OR MAYBE THEY JUST NEED MORE TIME.

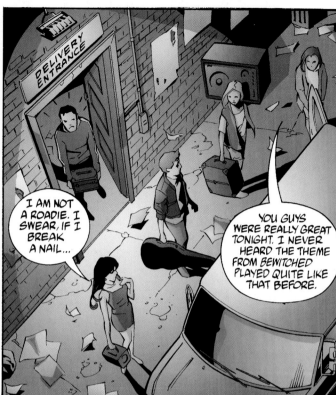

I AM NOT A ROADIE. I SWEAR, IF I BREAK A NAIL...

YOU GUYS WERE REALLY GREAT TONIGHT. I NEVER HEARD THE THEME FROM *BEWITCHED* PLAYED QUITE LIKE THAT BEFORE.

GLAD YOU LIKED IT. IT WAS FOR YOU.

WOW, THAT LITTLE NOISE YOU JUST HEARD? THAT WAS ME TRYING NOT TO EMBARRASS MYSELF BY SQUEALING WITH DELIGHT.

I KINDA LIKE WHEN YOU SQUEAL.

BOY, TOUGH CROWD IN THERE TONIGHT, THOUGH. MAYBE NOT LYNCH MOB, BUT DEFINITELY GRUMPY MOB.

YEAH. WELL, YOU AND BUFFY HAVE THAT *THEORY*...

OR MAYBE *NOT* A THEORY...

CRAP...

...THEY'RE FAST.

AND ALSO ...GROSS.

I JUST CAN'T BELIEVE IT. XANDER AND BUFFY WERE RIGHT!

I KNOW. IT'S JUST...VIDAL WOULD NEVER DO ANYTHING BAD.

YUP. THOSE POOR LITTLE GUYS MUST'VE JUST FALLEN IN WITH THE WRONG CROWD

I'M THINKING EXTERMINATOR.

OR THE NEXT BEST THING.

NOK NOK

HOLD ON, HOLD ON. DON'T GET YOUR KNICKERS IN A TWIST.

BUFFY? DO YOU HAVE ANY IDEA WHAT--

...I CONFESS I NEVER DREAMED I'D SEE ONE OF THESE. THE JAPANESE CALLED THEM BAKEMONO, BUT MOST OF THE LEGENDS COME FROM GERMANY, WHERE THEY WERE CALLED BAUMESEL.

NASTY LITTLE GITS. DIDN'T THINK THERE WERE ANY LEFT IN THIS DIMENSION, THEY'RE REPUTED TO MAKE THEIR HOMES IN THE HOLLOWS OF TREES. WITH THEIR MOTHER, OF COURSE.

TOY? I DON'T THINK SO.

ANY IDEA WHAT THIS THING IS?

THEIR MOTHER?

HOOLIGAN HOVEL? IT'S REALLY SORT OF QUAINT WHEN YOU THINK ABOUT IT.

WE'LL SEE HOW QUAINT YOU THINK THEY ARE WHEN THEY'RE MANIPULATING YOUR EMOTIONS, OR EVEN BETTER, SPITTING ON YOU.

OH, YOU'VE GOTTA BE KIDDING ME.

WELL, NOW IT ALL BEGINS TO MAKE SENSE.

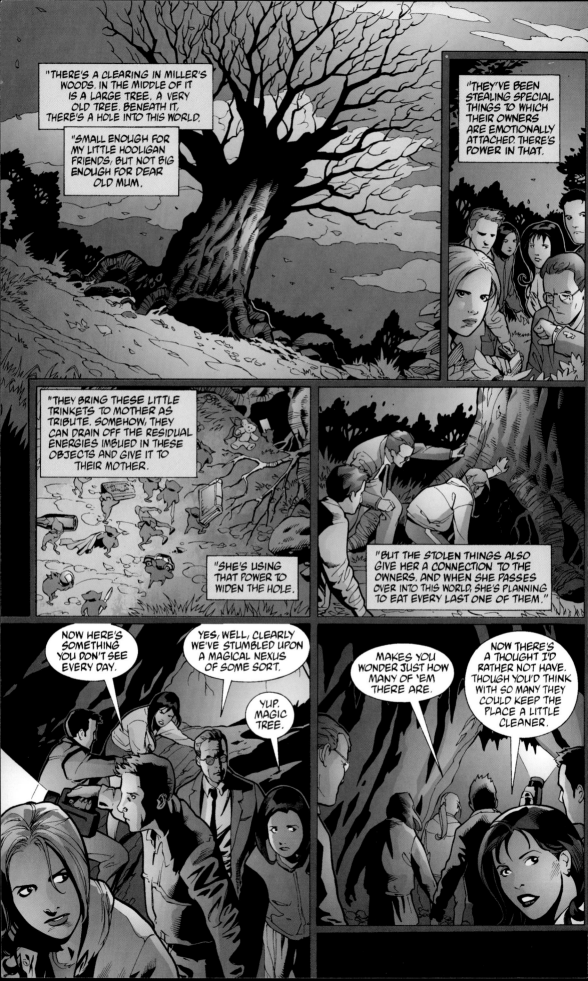

"THERE'S A CLEARING IN MILLER'S WOODS. IN THE MIDDLE OF IT IS A LARGE TREE. A VERY OLD TREE. BENEATH IT, THERE'S A HOLE INTO THIS WORLD.

"SMALL ENOUGH FOR MY LITTLE HOOLIGAN FRIENDS, BUT NOT BIG ENOUGH FOR DEAR OLD MUM.

"THEY'VE BEEN STEALING SPECIAL THINGS TO WHICH THEIR OWNERS ARE EMOTIONALLY ATTACHED. THERE'S POWER IN THAT.

"THEY BRING THESE LITTLE TRINKETS TO MOTHER AS TRIBUTE. SOMEHOW, THEY CAN DRAIN OFF THE RESIDUAL ENERGIES IMBUED IN THESE OBJECTS AND GIVE IT TO THEIR MOTHER.

"SHE'S USING THAT POWER TO WIDEN THE HOLE.

"BUT THE STOLEN THINGS ALSO GIVE HER A CONNECTION TO THE OWNERS, AND WHEN SHE PASSES OVER INTO THIS WORLD, SHE'S PLANNING TO EAT EVERY LAST ONE OF THEM."

NOW HERE'S SOMETHING YOU DON'T SEE EVERY DAY.

YES, WELL, CLEARLY WE'VE STUMBLED UPON A MAGICAL NEXUS OF SOME SORT.

YUP. MAGIC TREE.

MAKES YOU WONDER JUST HOW MANY OF 'EM THERE ARE.

NOW THERE'S A THOUGHT I'D RATHER NOT HAVE, THOUGH YOU'D THINK WITH SO MANY THEY COULD KEEP THE PLACE A LITTLE CLEANER.

AAAHHHH YAHHH!

HUJIXCL YJEQOPL FXUVPUYL!

HUJIXCL YJEQOPL FXUVPUYL!

HUJIXCL YJEQOPL FXUVPUYL!

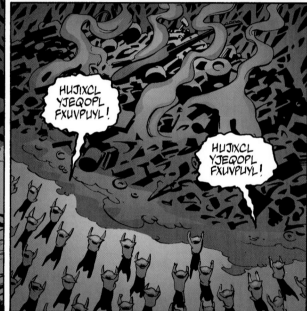

HUJIXCL YJEQOPL FXUVPUYL!

HUJIXCL YJEQOPL FXUVPUYL!

Y'KNOW, NOT THAT IT ISN'T A HEARTWARMING SPRINGER MOMENT TO SEE A MOTHER REUNITED WITH HER KIDS...

...BUT YOU AND YOUR LITTLE THIEVES DON'T BELONG HERE.

YEEE-ARRR!

...YYEEE-ARRRR...

HEY, OZ... WHY DON'T YOU PUT THIS SOMEWHERE SO IT DOESN'T GET BROKEN.

LOOK! PEZ WITCH!

YOU LITTLE MONSTERS! GET OFF ME. I SEE MY *GUCCI* BAG OVER THERE! I WAS WONDERING WHAT HAPPENED TO THAT.

I DIDN'T REALIZE THERE'D BE SO MANY OF THEM IN A SINGLE NEST.

YEAH. FASCINATING.

YAHHR

Stake out these Angel and Buffy the Vampire Slayer graphic novels

AUTUMNAL

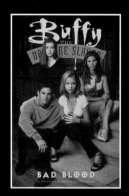

BAD BLOOD

the blood of carthage

CRASH TEST DEMONS

false Memories

FOOD CHAIN

HAUNTED

NOTE FROM THE UNDERGROUND

OUT OF THE WOODWORK

OZ

PALE REFLECTIONS

ANGEL

PAST LIVES

the REMAINING SUNLIGHT

Ugly Little Monsters

Uninvited Guests

ANGEL

Surrogates